Anonymous

Where can I Get a Car?

A street car directory of the city of Boston and surroundings

Anonymous

Where can I Get a Car?
A street car directory of the city of Boston and surroundings

ISBN/EAN: 9783337191702

Printed in Europe, USA, Canada, Australia, Japan

Cover: Foto ©Andreas Hilbeck / pixelio.de

More available books at **www.hansebooks.com**

Where CAN I GET A Car?

A STREET CAR DIRECTORY

... OF THE

CITY OF BOSTON

AND SURROUNDINGS

COMPRISING THE CITIES OF LYNN, SALEM, CAMBRIDGE, SOMERVILLE, MALDEN, EVERETT, WALTHAM, NEWTON, QUINCY, ROXBURY, WOBURN, CHELSEA AND MEDFORD; AND TOWNS OF WEYMOUTH, REVERE, SAUGUS, MELROSE, WAKEFIELD, STONEHAM, READING, MARBLEHEAD, SWAMPSCOTT, PEABODY, DANVERS, BEVERLY, WENHAM, HAMILTON, ETC., ETC.

Also, the Distant Lines Connecting with

ESTER, ROCKPORT, PLUM ISLAND, NEWBURYAMESBURY, SALISBURY BEACH, HAVERHIL,
RENCE, LOWELL, NATICK AND FRAMINGHAM.

GIVING

ections, Terminal Points, Fares, Transfers, etc.

Compiled and Copyright, 1894, by
T. W. PRESTON.

PUBLISHED BY
THE NICHOLS PRESS — THOS. P. NICHOLS.
LYNN, MASS.

TO THE PUBLIC.

—— ——

THE oft-asked question, where can I get a car for this or that place or point, not only by the stranger or visitor from out of town, but residents, business men and natives of the City of Boston, has never been satisfactorily answered, and until now they were in doubt whether the car they want is to be had on Scollay Square, Rowe's Wharf, or Boylston Street, frequently being obliged to hire a herdic, or pay two fares, where one would do if properly informed, besides the delay and vexatious loss of time.

My book, "Where to Go — How to Get There," (now considered the banner Guide-Book of Boston and surroundings), which has given such unbounded satisfaction, is intended as a path-finder for visitors and pleasure seekers. In this work I intend, in brief form, and more extended in usefulness, a hand-book that will help the business men and general public to unravel the complicated street-car system of Boston and surrounding cities and towns. As changes and extensions are made I will be prepared in each succeeding edition to map out, and explain in complete detail, the network of electric railroads that are fast spreading over and through our cities, towns and outlying country, which afford pleasure, convenience and cheapness of travel to the masses, in the form of the poor man's carriage.

While soliciting a generous patronage, I also invite honest criticism from the press and public, hoping to merit your favors.

I am yours truly,

T. W. PRESTON.

October, 1894.

WHERE CAN I GET A CAR?

E WILL first show by certain colors what district of **Boston,** or particular suburb, a car belongs; next (under "Location" and number), we will place ourselves on a designated point, and note every car going right or left, giving number of cars per hour, general direction, and destination; then we will show, in alphabetical order, as per index, routes, destinations, etc. Next, we cross the country north and east through towns and cities to the bank of the Merrimac River, taking in the distant points of Gloucester, Rockport, Newburyport, and passing through Amesbury, Haverhill, and Lawrence to Lowell, which will soon be connected with Boston.

In classifying the street cars in the City of Boston, we will begin with those of the Lynn & Boston Railroad Company, which enter the city from Charlestown via Warren Bridge, near Union Station, and through Beverly Street, Haymarket Square, Sudbury Street to Scollay Square, and returning via Cornhill, Adams Square, Washington Street, Haymarket Square and Beverly Street to Warren Bridge, etc. All other cars belong to the West End Railroad Company, and are classed as follows in

DISTINCTIVE COLORS.

Dark Blue Cars.—All Dorchester cars, except those for Mt. Bowdoin (marked *Grove Hall, Dorchester*); one line terminates at Union Station, and via Washington

St. and Dorchester Ave. to Field's Corner. The three
remaining lines enter the city by Washington St. to
Franklin St., passing down to Chauncy St., and by Sum-
mer St. to Washington St., and via Northampton St.,
Hampden St., and Mt. Pleasant to Milton, Neponset or
Meeting-house Hill.

Light Blue Cars. — (Via Huntington Ave.) Leave
points between Union Station and Tremont House via
Sudbury St., going southwest and west. The Park St.
line is extended to the Reservoir. All cars on East Boston side from ferry to Bellingham, Chelsea, Orient Heights
and Lexington St.

Lemon Yellow Cars. — Columbus Ave. or Tremont St. are principally to Roxbury points. The amber
cars of Roxbury and Charlestown line pass through Columbus Ave. via Warren St. to Grove Hall, and a lemon
yellow line from Lenox St. via Columbus Ave, Park and
Scollay Sqs., through Charlestown to Davis Sq., West
Somerville, and one from Chelsea Ferry to Old Heath St.

Amber Yellow Cars. — (Charlestown via Warren
Bridge.) All cars for Medford, Malden, Everett, West
Everett, Somerville (via Charlestown) or Bunker Hill are
amber color, except one line to Grove Hall, via Washing-
ton St. and Blue Hill Ave. There is an amber line in
Cambridge, marked *Cambridge Circuit.*

Dark Green Cars. — (Shawmut Ave. and Washington St.) The course of these lines are southwest, except the Cross Town, which goes a Z course, taking the
Back Bay Columbus Ave., Northampton and Dudley Sts.
to Blue Hill Ave. and Grove Hall, a green line from
Chelsea Ferry, and the Grove Hall, Dorchester.

Scarlet Cars. — (South Boston.) Cars from City Point, marked *South Boston* on dasher, leave the city from Union Station via Washington St ; from Park Sq. via Columbus Ave. to Berkeley St. and Dover St. Those via Scollay Sq. enter Tremont St., going north from Temple Place, passing the Winthrop monument at the south end of Scollay Sq. to Cornhill, returning to South Boston via Washington St. There is a scarlet line from City Point, marked *Cambridge and South Boston*, to Harvard Sq., and a line from Union Station, Causeway St. and Atlantic Ave. to Rowe's Wharf, and Federal and Summer Sts. to Albany and Old Colony Depots, Kneeland St.

Crimson Cars. — (Cambridge.) All cars between the different points of Boston and Cambridge, and all cars passing through Cambridgeport or East Cambridge to Brighton, Somerville. Arlington, Newton or Watertown are dark red or crimson. There is also a line to City Point from Harvard Sq.

Chocolate Colored Cars. — (Brighton.) Two lines to Oak Sq. and Allston, and one to the Reservoir are this color.

Pea Green Cars. — (Back Bay.) See Back Bay.

Pale Yellow Cars. — When the electric lines in East Boston are complete, the color will be changed from the present blue to an écru shade.

CONNECTIONS.

The cars of the West End Co., of Boston, connect with Lynn & Boston R. R., at Bellingham (Chelsea), Malden Sq. (Malden), Main St. and Everett Sq. (Everett), Medford Sq. (Medford) and between Bunker Hill St. (Charlestown) and Scollay Sq., Cornhill or Adams Sq.

At Newton Corner or Watertown, with crimson cars for Waltham, Newtonville and West Newton.

At Neponset, with amber cars for Quincy via Norfolk Downs and Wollaston Heights, West Quincy, Hough's Neck, Quincy Point, North Weymouth and East Weymouth.

The Lynn & Boston R.R. Co., with West End R. R. as above, and at Lynnhurst. Stoneham and Melrose with Wakefield & Stoneham St. R.R. Amber cars.

FARES.

All fares on the West End cars are on the five-cent basis, except to Arlington, Newton, Watertown or West Medford, and to Medford Sq. via Malden.

Fares on other roads will be shown in alphabetical list of routes.

On all street cars, it is better to pay 5-cent fares, which carry you from boundary to boundary besides giving you the benefit of any transfers which are issued, which I will here illustrate.

The schedule fare on the cars from Woburn to Salem via Melrose is 30 cents, with 5 cents additional to Beverly or the Willows. On leaving Woburn, 5 cents carries you to the Stoneham and Melrose boundary. Your next 5-cent fare gives you a transfer to the Saugus and Melrose boundary. (This transfer is required on account of changing to the Lynn and Salem car at Melrose car shed.) Your next 5-cent fare carries you through Saugus, Lynn and Upper Swampscott to the Lynn and Salem boundary. When you are called on for your next fare (5 cents) you are in South Salem, and entitled to a transfer to North Salem, Beverly or the Willows, in all 20 cents, showing a saving of 15 cents. There is nothing illegal or deceptive about this mode of paying fares.

TRANSFERS.

Boston. — Stop-over transfer checks are issued by the West End R.R. Co. under the following directions: Price 8 cents, good only on day of issue. Red check (forenoon) for morning or forenoon is issued up to 11.30, A.M., and is good to 1, P.M. Blue check (afternoon) is good any time during afternoon and evening of day of issue.

Free transfer tickets are provided by car starters at the following points, in extension of present ride in same general direction, and used only at place of issue: Harvard Sq., Craigie's Bridge, West Boston Bridge (Cambridge side), Grove Hall, both ends of North Ferry to East Boston, cor. Dudley and Washington Sts. and West Broadway, South Boston.

Conductors give free checks at Mt. Auburn and North Ave., to be exchanged for an inward check at Harvard Sq., if required. This is done to prevent 5-cent passengers from Watertown, Newton or Arlington getting a free ride to Boston.

Lynn. — The Lynn & Boston R.R. issue free transfers to boundaries on 5-cent rides in all cities and towns when two or more of their lines pass thr'ough, excepting Lynn, where a transfer is good from the outside boundaries of Swampscott, through Lynn, to the farthest boundary of Saugus, excepting North Saugus, which is operated by the Wakefield Co. All 5-cent rides in the city of Lynn and towns of Swampscott and Saugus allow transfers to Nahant beach, excepting the Belt Line circuit, which only transfers to a Boston car.

Wakefield. — Free transfers are given to Melrose or to Reading boundary.

Watertown. — Leaving Watertown for Newtonville you can get a 7-cent transfer check to Newton Upper Falls and Echo Bridge Park.

Quincy. — The Quincy & Boston R. R. Co. issue 8-cent checks from Neponset to West Quincy, Neponset to Quincy Point, and Quincy Point to West Quincy.

Revere and Chelsea. — The Lynn & Boston R.R. give 8-cent transfers on Revere and Chelsea cars ; and the West End R.R. also extend their 8-cent checks to Lynn & Boston cars.

Linden. — Passengers on Lynn & Boston R.R. cars for Linden or Revere Beach will require checks for the transfer car.

All Transfer Checks must be asked for on payment of fare.

Location 1.

A person at SCOLLAY SQUARE can take cars to

	Cars per Hour	Direction Going
† City Point	12	N E
Forest Hills (via Shawmut Ave.) . . .	6	S
Green St. (via Shawmut Ave.)	16	S
Grove Hall (via Huntington Ave. Cross Town)	3	S
Grove Hall (via Columbus Ave.) . . .	6	S
Grove Hall (via Shawmut Ave.) . . .	6	S
Dudley St. (via Shawmut Ave.)	16	
* Lenox St. (via Tremont St.)	32	
* Roxbury Crossing (via Tremont St.)	28	
* Old Heath St. (via Tremont St.) . .	15	
Jamaica Plain (via Tremont St.) . . .	8	
Brookline (via Tremont St.)	6	
Columbus Ave. to Northampton St.	22	
Huntington Ave. to Massachusetts Ave.	15	
Marlboro St. (via Back Bay)	4	
City Sq., Charlestown	64	
Bunker Hill	6	
Charlestown Neck	52	
Magoun Sq., Somerville	6	
Central St., Somerville	6	
* Davis Sq.	4	
Union Sq., (via Charlestown)	12	
Everett, B. & M. Crossing	28	
Everett Sq.	12	
Malden (via Everett Sq. to W. Everett)	4	

† Go via Cornhill at the Monument.
* Go via Hanover Street.

	Cars per Hour	Direction Going
West Everett	8	
Winter Hill	6	
Medford (via Winter Hill)	6	
Malden (via Broadway, Everett) . . .	4	
East Cambridge	16	
Central Sq., Cambridgeport	4	
Baldwin St.	8	
Harvard Sq., (via East Cambridge) . .	4	
Union Sq. (via East Cambridge) . . .	4	
* East Boston Ferry	20	
* Chelsea Ferry	4	
Union Station	65	
Chelsea Sq.	20	
Washington Ave.	8	
Woodlawn Cemetery	2	
Beachmont	2	
Crescent Beach	6	
Lynn	4	
Swampscott	4	
Marblehead	2	
Revere Beach, summer line, connecting with Lynn cars by transfer (free) .	2	
Linden, free transfer from Lynn car . .	2	

* Go via Hanover Street.

All Lynn and Boston cars, and all West End cars, not otherwise specified, pass through the Square from Sudbury Street to Cornhill to Adams Square.

Location 2.

A person at **BOWDOIN SQUARE** can take cars to

Marlboro' St. and Massachusetts Ave.	3	W
Oak Sq., Brighton and Allston	4	W
Harvard Sq.	17	W

	Cars per Hour	Direction Going
Newton	4	W
Mt. Auburn	4	W
Broadway, Cambridge	4	W
Arlington and Arlington Heights	4	W
North Ave.	10	W
Porter's Station	4	W
Summer St.	5	W
Union Station	3	N
Brighton, Western Ave.		W

Location 3.

A person at **POST OFFICE SQUARE** can take cars to

City Point	6	S
Baldwin St. and East Cambridge	6	N
City Sq., Charlestown	20	N
Charlestown Neck	14	N
Bunker Hill	6	N
Winter Hill	8	N
Franklin St., Somerville	6	N
Columbus Ave., to Northampton St.	6	S
Union Station	53	N
East Boston Ferry	15	N

Location 4.

A Person on **TREMONT STREET**, between **TRE-MONT HOUSE** and **BOYLSTON STREET**, can take cars to

City Point	12	N*
Forest Hills (via. Shawmut Ave.)	6	S

* From Temple Place.

	Cars per Hour	Direction Going
Green St.	16	S
Grove Hall (via Huntington Ave.—Cross Town)	6	S
Grove Hall (via Columbus Ave.) . . .	6	S
Grove Hall (via Shawmut Ave.) . . .	6	S
Dudley St. (via Shawmut Ave.) . . .	22	S
Lenox St. (via Tremont St.)	52	S
Roxbury Crossing (via Tremont St.) .	48	S
Old Heath St. (via Tremont St.) . . .	27	S
Jamaica Plain (via Tremont St.) . . .	20	S
Brookline (via Tremont St.) . . .	6	S
Columbus Ave. to Northampton St. . .	22	S
Huntington Ave. to cor. Mass. Ave. .	35	S
Huntington Ave. to Cypress St., Brookline	7	S
Huntington Ave. to Park St., Brookline	7	S
Huntington Ave. to Longwood, Brookline	3	S
Boylston St., to cor. Massachusetts Ave.	32	S
Main cor. Pearl St., Cambridge . . .	14	S
Harvard Sq. (via Harvard Bridge) . .	12	S
Coolidge's Corner, Brookline	18	S
Reservoir	6	S
Allston (Brighton)	12	S
Oak Sq.	6	S
Marlboro St. (via Back Bay)	4	S
City Sq., Charlestown	30	N
Bunker Hill	6	N
Charlestown Neck	24	N
Magoun Sq., Somerville	6	N
Central St., Somerville	6	N
Davis Sq., Somerville	4	N
Union Sq., Somerville	12	N
East Boston Ferry	20	N

	Cars per Hour	Direction Going
Chelsea Ferry	4	N
Union Station	65	N
Longwood	3	S

Location 5.

A person at **HAYMARKET SQUARE** can take cars to

Grove Hall and Franklln Park	18
Norfolk House	8
Field's Corner	8
Milton	2
City Point	16
Albany & O. C. Depots	16
City Square, Charlestown	50
Bunker Hill	12
Union Square	12
Winter Hill	12
Medford	6
Malden	10
West Everett	8
Everett Square	14
Jamaica Plain	6

Location 6.

A person at **PARK SQUARE** can take cars to

Union Station	22	N
Grove Hall	12	W
Davis Sq., West Somerville	4	N

	Cars per Hour	Direction Going
Reservoir.	6	W
Albany and O. C. Depots	6	S W
Brookline Village	8	W
Oak Sq., Brighton	6	W
Allston.	12	W
Harvard Sq., ...	12	N
Pearl St., Cambridgeport.	2	N
Clarendon Hill.	4	N
Spring Hill	2	N
City Point	10	S W
City Sq., Charlestown	4	N
Field's Corner	4	
Scollay Sq.	34	N
Longwood	3	W
Coolidge's Corner	18	W

Location 7.

A person at **COPLEY SQUARE** can take cars to

Grove Hall	6	W
Reservoir	6	W
Brookline Village	8	W
Oak Square, Brighton	6	W
Allston	12	W
Harvard Sq.	12	W
Pearl St., Cambridgeport.	2	W
Field's Corner	4	W
Longwood	3	W
Scollay Sq.	12	E
Coolidge's Corner	18	W

Location 8.

A person on **WASHINGTON STREET**, between **BOYLSTON STREET** and **CORNHILL**, can take cars to

	Cars per Hour	Direction Going
City Point (via Broadway)	18	S
City Point (via Bay View)	12	S
Albany and O. C. Depots	55	S
N. Y. & N. E. Depot	28	S
Cor. Broadway and Dorchester Ave.	47	S
Dorchester St., South Boston	27	.S
Dudley St., (via Washington St.)	59	S
Franklin Park	12*	S
Grove Hall (via Washington Street and Warren Street)	18	S
Grove Hall (via Blue Hill Ave.)	12	S
Dorchester (via Grove Hall)	6	S
Norfolk House	8	S
Bartlett St.	23	S
Roxbury Crossing	8	S
Upham's Corner	20	S
Field's Corner (via Mt. Pleasant)	14	S
Milton (via Mt. Pleasant)	6	S
Neponset (via Mt. Pleasant)	4	S
Meeting House Hill	6	S
Field's Corner (via Dorchester Ave.)	16	S
Milton (via Dorchester Ave.)	4	S
Neponset (via Dorchester Ave.)	4	S
Rowe's Wharf	16	N†
Bowdoin Sq. and West End	6	N

* Sundays 22.
† North of Summer Street.

	Cars per Hour	Direction Going
City Sq., Charlestown	36	N
Bunker Hill	12	N
Charlestown Neck	24	N
Franklin St., Somerville	14	N
Winter Hill, Somerville	8	N
Union Sq., Somerville	12	N
East Cambridge	6	N
East Boston Ferry	15	N
Union Station	69	N

Location 9.

A person at **CITY SQUARE**, Charlestown, can take cars to

Union Sq.	12
Davis Sq.	6
Magoun Sq.	4
Winter Hill	12
Medford	6
Malden	10
West Everett	8
Everett Sq.	14
Bunker Hill	12
Grove Hall	6
Columbus Ave.	4
Tremont St. to Lenox St.	4
Union Station	60
Albany and O. C. Depots	12
Park Sq.	4
Chelsea Sq.	20
Washington Ave.	8

Woodlawn Cemetery 2
Beachmont 2
Crescent Beach 6
Lynn 4
Swampscott 4
Marblehead 2
Revere Beach, transfer from Lynn car . . . 2
Linden, transfer from Lynn car 2

Location 10.

A person at **OLD COLONY** and **ALBANY DE-POTS** can take cars to

City Point (via Broadway) 18
City Point (via Bay View) 8
Rowe's Wharf (during summer months) . . . 8
Columbus Ave. 6
Bunker Hill and Navy Yard 6
Winter Hill 6
Union Station 29
City Sq., Charlestown 12

Location 11.

A person at **UNION STATION** can take cars to

Grove Hall (via Warren St.) 9
Grove Hall (via Hampden St.) 6
Norfolk House 6
Forest Hills 6
Milton 2
Field's Corner (via Washington St.) 4

	Cars per Hour
Field's Corner (via Dorchester Ave.)	4
Rowe's Wharf, during summer months	8
Jamaica Plain	6
Columbus Ave.	10
Huntington Ave.	12
Longwood Ave.	3
Brookline, by free transfer at Roxbury Crossing	6
Tremont St., as far as Lenox St.	16
City Point (via Broadway)	12
City Point (via Bay View)	4
Harvard Sq.	4
East Cambridge	12
Spring Hill, Somerville	2
Winter Hill	12
Bunker Hill	12
Davis Sq., West Somerville	6
Magoun Sq., West Somerville	4
Medford	6
Malden	10
Everett (East and West)	22
City Sq., Charlestown	60
Park Sq. and Providence Depot	10

Location 12.

A person at **ROWE'S WHARF** can take cars to

Union Station	8
Albany and O. C. Depots	8
Roxbury Crossing	6
Bartlett St., Roxbury	6

Location 13.

A person at **HARVARD SQUARE** can take cars to

Cars per Hour

Bowdoin Sq.	12
Tremont House	12
Arlington Heights	4
North Ave.	8
Newton and Mt. Auburn	4
Huron Ave.	3
East Cambridge	4
City Point	
Park Sq.	12

Location 14.

A person at **WEST LENOX STREET**, corner **TREMONT**, can take cars to

Jamaica Plain	12
East Boston Ferry	16
Union Station	14
Rowe's Wharf	15

Location 15.

A person at **ROXBURY CROSSING** can take cars to

East Boston Ferry	16
Union Station	6
Brookline Village	6
Rowe's Wharf	16

Location 16.

A person at corner of **DUDLEY** and **WASHINGTON STREETS** can take cars to

Cars
per Hour

Grove Hall	15
Dorchester	6
Field's Corner	15
Forest Hills	6
Egleston Sq.	12
Union Station	22
Scollay Sq.	9

Location 17.

A person at **UPHAM'S CORNER** can take cars to

Field's Corner	12
Meeting House Hill	6
Union Station	4
Franklin St.	18
Neponset	2
Milton	4

Location 18.

A person at **BROADWAY, South Boston,** can take cars to

Union Station	16
Scollay Sq.	12
Albany and Old Colony Depots	22
City Point	16
Post Office Sq.	20
Harvard Sq.	8

Location 19.

A person at **COOLIDGE'S CORNER** can take cars to

	Cars per Hour
Oak Sq.	6
Reservoir	6
Allston	10
Tremont House	16

Location 20.

A person at **MEDFORD SQUARE** can take cars to

Scollay Sq.	6
Malden	2
Everett Sq.	2
West Everett	2
West Medford	2
City Sq., Charlestown	6

Location 21.

A person at **MALDEN STATION** can take cars to

Scollay Sq. (via Ferry St. and Broadway)	6
Scollay Sq. (via West Everett)	4

Location 22.

A person at **EVERETT SQUARE** can take cars to

Scollay Sq. (via Charlestown Neck)	12
* Chelsea	2

* Lynn & Boston R.R.

Location 23.

A person at **CRAIGIE'S BRIDGE** can take cars to

Cars
per Hour

Harvard Sq. (via Cambridge St., E. Cambridge) 4
Central Sq. and Riverside 4
Union Sq. and Spring Hill 2
Clarendon Hill, West Somerville 4
Park Sq. 4
Union Station 12
Scollay Sq. 8
South Boston 6

Location 24.

A person at **WEST BOSTON BRIDGE** can take cars to

Harvard Sq. . . . . : 24
Newton and Mt. Auburn 4
Arlington Heights 4
North Avenue 8
Oak Sq., Brighton 4
Allston 4
Riverside 8
Cottage Farm 2
Bowdoin Sq. 25
Park Sq. 8
South Boston 8
Spring Hill 4
Broadway, Cambridge 4

Location 25.

A person at **SULLIVAN SQUARE**, **Charlestown,** can take cars to

	Cars per Hour
West Somerville	6
Magoun Sq.	4
Winter Hill	14
Union Sq.	6
Medford	6
Malden	10
Everett Sq.	15
West Everett	4
Union Station	48
Tremont House	10
Park Sq.	6
Scollay Sq.	39
Grove Hall	6
Dudley St.	12
Albany and Old Colony Depots	5

Location 26.

A person at **BUNKER HILL** can take cars to

Albany and Old Colony Depots	6
Grove Hall	6
Temple Place	12
Union Station	12

Location 27.

A person at **NORTH FERRY, East Boston,** can take cars to

Chelsea	6
Lexington St.	6

	Cars per Hour
Winthrop	6
Jeffries' Point	4
Bartlett St. (via Washington St., City) . . .	12
Roxbury Crossing (City)	15
Scollay Sq. (City)	15

Location 28.

A person at CENTRAL SQUARE, East Boston, can take cars to

Chelsea	6
Lexington St.	6
Winthrop	6
Bartlett St. (via Washington St., City.) . .	12
Roxbury Crossing (City)	15
Scollay Sq. (City)	15
Temple Place (cor. Washington St., City) .	12

Location 29.

A person at MALDEN SQUARE can take cars to

Chelsea	2 in A.M., 4 in P.M.
Melrose Highlands	2 in A.M., 4 in P.M.
Stoneham	2
Woburn	2
Maplewood and Linden	2
Lynn and Salem (via Upper Swampscott) . .	1
Pine Banks Park	2 in A.M., 4 in P.M.
Melrose	2 in A.M., 4 in P.M.
Franklin Park, Saugus	1
Cliftondale	1

Location 30.

A person at **CHELSEA SQUARE** can take cars to

Cars per Hour

Washington Ave.	8
Woodlawn Cemetery	2
Beachmont	2
Crescent Beach	6
Lynn, Revere and Linden	4
Lower Swampscott	4
Marblehead	2
Everett Sq.	2
Malden	2 in A.M., 4 in P.M.
Melrose Highlands	2 in A.M., 4 in P.M.
Stoneham	2
Woburn	2
Melrose	2

Location 31.

A person at **STONEHAM SQUARE** can take cars to

Woburn	2
Melrose Highlands	2
Malden	2
Everett	2
Chelsea	2

Location 32.

A person at **DEPOT SQUARE, Woburn,** can take cars to

Stoneham	2
Melrose Highlands	2

	Cars per Hour
Malden	2
Everett	2
Chelsea	2
North Woburn	1
Winchester	1
Medford Sq.	1

Location 33.

A person at MELROSE CAR SHED can take cars to

Woburn	2
Stoneham	2
Wakefield	2
Reading	2
No. Saugus	2
Melrose Highlands	2
Malden	2
Chelsea	2
Everett	2
Stoneham (via Wakefield)	2
Lynn (via Wakefield)	2
Lynn (via Saugus Centre)	2
Salem	2
Upper Swampscott	2

Location 34.

A person at MARKET SQUARE, Lynn, can take cars to

Boston	4
Lynnhurst and Wakefield (via No. Saugus)	1
Belt Line	2

Central Depot 6
Marblehead 2
Wyoma (via Chestnut St.) 2
Glenmere (via Chestnut St.) 2
Lower Swampscott (via Broad and Lewis Sts.) 4

Location 35.

A person at **CITY HALL SQUARE, Lynn,** can take cars to

Boston 4
Myrtle St. (via Franklin St.) 4
Myrtle St. (via Walnut St.) 2
Wyoma and Peabody (via Washington St.) . 1
Wyoma (via Chestnut St.) 2
Wyoma (via Euclid Ave.) 2
Glenmere (via Chatham St.) 4
Glenmere (via Chestnut St.) 2
Marblehead 2
Lower Swampscott (via Broad and Lewis Sts.) 4
Lewis St. (via Market and Broad Sts.) . . . 1
Nahant Beach 1
Highland Circuit 3

Location 36.

A person at **CENTRAL SQUARE, Lynn,** can take cars to

Boston 4
Malden (via Franklin Park, Linden and Maplewood 1

	Cars per Hour
Melrose, Stoneham and Woburn	1
Cliftondale	2
Saugus Centre	2
Myrtle St. (via Franklin St.)	4
Lynnhurst, No. Saugus and Wakefield	1
Myrtle St. (via Walnut St.)	1
Wyoma and Peabody (via Washington St.)	1
Wyoma (via Chestnut St.)	2
Wyoma (via Euclid Ave.)	2
Glenmere (via Chatham St.)	4
Glenmere (via Chestnut St.)	2
Glenmere (via Laighton St.)	2
Glenmere (via Belt Line)	2
Salem	4
Upper Swampscott (via Timson St.)	2
Upper Swampscott (via Essex St.)	2
Marblehead	2
Lower Swampscott (via Broad and Lewis St.)	4
Nahant Beach	1

Location 37.

A person at **TOWN HOUSE SQUARE**, Salem, can take cars to

Peabody	1
Danvers Centre	1
Putnamville	1
Danvers Sq.	4
Marblehead Fort	4
Willows (via Derby St.)	2
* Willows (via Essex St.)	2

* After 12.30 P.M.

Upper Swampscott 2

Lynn 2

Saugus Centre 2

Melrose 2

Stoneham and Woburn 2

Chapman's Corner, Beverly Cove 1

North Beverly and Wenham 1

Gloucester Crossing, Beverly 4

Location 38.

A person at the **MONUMENT** or **FORT SEWELL, Marblehead,** can take cars to

Salem and South Salem 4

Danvers 1

Asylum Station 1

North Salem and Danversport 1

Swampscott and Lynn 2

Revere, Chelsea and Boston . . . . : 2

Location 39.

A person at **GLOUCESTER CROSSING, BEVERLY SQUARE,** can take cars to

Salem (Town House Sq.) 4

Chapman's Corner, Beverly Cove 1

Peabody Sq. 1

Danvers and Putnamville 1

Wenham and Hamilton (Hamilton, summer
only) 1

Location 40.

A person at **PEABODY SQUARE** can take cars to

Lynn and Wyoma 1
Salem and Beverly (via Essex St) 2
Danvers and Putnamville 1
Willows 1
North Salem 2

Location 41.

A person at **CITY HALL SQUARE, Quincy,**
can take cars to

Neponset 2
West Quincy 2
Quincy Point 2
East Weymouth 2
Hough's Neck (summer line) . . . .

INDEX OF ROUTES

OF THE

West End, Quincy and Boston, Newton, Newton and Boston, and Watertown and Newtonville Street Railway Companies, radiating from Scollay Square, Boston.

———— · ——

Albany and Old Colony Depots (Kneeland St.). *Red car*—from Union Station, via Causeway St. and Atlantic Ave. *Amber car*—from Bunker Hill, and all South Boston cars, except Broadway extension. See Locations **5, 6, 8, 9, 12, 18, 25, 26**

Allston. *Chocolate car* — at Tremont House, via Tremont and Boylston Sts., Massachusetts Ave. and Beacon St. to Coolidge's Cor. and Harvard Ave. *Chocolate car*—from Bowdoin Sq. and West Boston Bridge, Main and River Sts., Cambridgeport. See Locations **2, 3, 6, 7, 19**

Arlington and Arlington Heights. *Crimson car*—at Bowdoin Sq., cor. Green St., via West Boston Bridge, Main St., Harvard Sq. and North Ave. See Locations **2, 13, 24**

Ashmont and Milton. *Dark Blue car*—from Union Station and Franklin St., via Washington St., or Dorchester Ave. See Locations **5, 8**

Back Bay (Union Station line). *Pale Green car*—from Washington and Northampton Sts., and runs via Northampton St., Columbus Ave., Massachusetts Ave., Marlboro St., Arlington St., Beacon St., Charles St., Cambridge St., Bowdoin Sq., Green St., Staniford St., Causeway St., returning, via Portland St., Chardon St., Bowdoin Sq., Green St., Chambers St., Cambridge St., thence same route. See Locations **2, 11**

Baldwin Street—see *East Cambridge*.

Bartlett Street—see *Highlands*.

Bowdoin Square. Terminus of cars from Cambridge, Somerville, Arlington and Newton. Route of Back Bay and Belt Line.   See Locations **13, 24**

Brighton.

OAK SQUARE. Terminus of Allston and Brighton car. (One of the longest rides from Boston).
See Locations **2, 4, 6, 7, 19, 24**

WESTERN AVE. *Crimson car*—from Bowdoin Sq., via Cambridgeport.   See Location **2**

Broadway — see *Cambridge, Chelsea, Everett, South Boston*.

Brookline. *Blue car*—from Tremont House, via Boylston St. and Huntington Ave., also Reservoir and Allston cars.   See Locations **1, 4, 6, 7, 11, 15**

Bunker Hill. *Amber car* — from Grove Hall, via Warren St.; Albany and Old Colony Depots; Scollay Sq. *Green car*—from Grove Hall, via Blue Hills Ave. See Locations **1, 3, 4, 5, 8, 9, 10, 11, 26**

Cambridge.

BROADWAY. *Crimson car* — from Bowdoin Sq. to Harvard Sq.   See Locations **2, 24**

CAMBRIDGE CIRCUIT. *Amber car*—from River St., Prospect St., Cambridge St., Harvard Sq., Main St., Pearl St., Putnam Ave.; Putnam Ave., Pearl St., Main St., Cambridge St., Prospect St., River St.

HARVARD SQUARE. *Crimson car* — marked *Cambridge* or *East Cambridge;* or Arlington, Mt. Auburn or Newton cars at Bowdoin Sq.; or *Red car* at City Point.
See Locations **1, 2, 3, 4, 6, 7, 11, 13, 18, 23, 24**

PEARL STREET AND PUTNAM AVENUE. *Crimson car*—via Back Bay and Harvard Bridge.
See Locations **4, 7**

Cambridge — *continued.*

SUMMER STREET. *Red car*—from Bowdoin Sq.
See Location **2**

Central Street — see *Somerville.*

Cambridgeport. CENTRAL SQUARE. Take any
Cambridge car except East Cambridge.

Central Square — see *Cambridgeport.*

Charlestown. CITY SQUARE. Take any Charlestown, Everett, Lynn, or Revere car.
See Locations **1, 3, 4, 5, 6, 8, 10, 11, 20**

Chelsea. BROADWAY. Any Chelsea, Revere, or
Lynn car. See Locations **1, 5**

Chelsea Ferry. *Green car* — on Washington or
Hanover Sts., or Chelsea Ferry cars.
See Locations **1, 4**

Chestnut Hill Reservoir. *Chocolate car* — on
Tremont or Boylston Sts., via Massachusetts Ave.
and Beacon St. *Light Blue car* — via Huntington
Ave. (old Park St. line). See Locations **6, 7**

City Point — see *South Boston.*

City Square — see *Charlestown.*

Clarendon Hill. *Crimson car* — from Park Sq.,
via Charles St. and Craigie's Bridge, Somerville
Ave., and Davis Square, West Somerville.
See Locations **6, 23**

Columbus Avenue. *Green* or *Yellow cars* —on
Tremont St. See Locations **1, 3, 4, 9, 10, 11**

Coolidge's Corner. Take Reservoir or Allston
car. See Locations **4, 6, 7, 19**

Davis Square. *Yellow car*—Highland Ave. *Red
car*—Clarendon Hill.
See Locations **1, 4, 6, 9, 11, 23**

Dorchester.
FIELD'S CORNER. *Dark Blue car*—at Franklin St.,
or Warren Bridge, via Mount Pleasant, or Dorchester Ave. See Locations **5, 8, 11, 16, 17**

Dorchester — *continued.*

FIELD'S CORNER. (Park Sq. Cross Town line), starts
from Park St. (Dorchester), via Dorchester Ave.,
Savin Hill Ave., Pleasant St., Stoughton St., Dudley St., Washington St., Northampton St., Columbus Ave., Massachusetts Ave., Huntington Ave.,
Boylston St., Church St., to Park Sq., returning
via Boylston St., thence same route.
See Locations **6, 7, 16**

GROVE HALL. *Green car*—via Warren and Washington Sts.   See Locations **5, 8, 9, 11**

Dorchester Street — see *South Boston.*

Dudley Street. Take any Mt. Pleasant, Grove
Hall, or Forest Hill car.
See Locations **1, 4, 8, 16, 25**

East Boston Ferry (377 Commercial St.). *Yellow car* — from Old Heath St. (Roxbury), via Tremont St., Scollay Sq. and Hanover St. *Green car*—
from Bartlett St. (Highlands), via Washington St.,
Temple Place, Tremont and Hanover Sts., to Ferry.
See Locations **1, 3, 4, 8, 14, 15**

East Cambridge. *Crimson car*—from City Point
or Scollay Sq., via Leverett St., Craigie's Bridge
and Cambridge St., East Cambridge.
See Locations **1, 3, 8, 11, 23**

BALDWIN STREET. *Crimson car*—Sudbury St. to
Scollay Sq. and Cornhill, to Washington St. and
Leverett St. to Craigie's Bridge.
See Locations **1, 3, 11**

East Somerville. WINTER HILL. *Amber car*—
north from Boylston St.
See Locations **1, 8, 9, 10, 11, 25**

East Weymouth. Terminus of Quincy cars from
Neponset, Quincy and Quincy Point. 5 cents from
latter place.   See Location **41**

Echo Bridge Park. *Scarlet car*—at Watertown
or Newtonville. See *Newton car.*

Everett.

BROADWAY. Take Everett car marked *Broadway*.
See Locations **1, 5, 21**

EVERETT SQUARE. *Amber car*—from Scollay Sq.,
via Warren Bridge and Charlestown.
See Locations **1, 5, 9, 11, 20, 25**

Field's Corner — see *Dorchester*.

Forest Hills. *Green car* — from Union Station,
via Tremont St., Shawmut Ave. and Washington
St., to Egleston Sq. See Locations **1, 4, 11, 16**

Franklin Park — see *West Roxbury*.

Franklin Street — see *Somerville*.

Green Street — see *Highlands*.

Grove Hall — see *Dorchester, Roxbury*.

Highlands.

BARTLETT STREET. *Green car*—from East Boston
North Ferry, via Washington St.
See Locations **8, 12**

GREEN STREET. *Green car*—from Chelsea Ferry,
or Forest Hills car. See Locations **1, 4**

Harvard Square — see *Cambridge*.

Hough's Neck — see *Quincy*.

Huntington Avenue. *Light Blue car* — from
Tremont St., or any car marked *Huntington Ave.*
See Locations **1, 4**

Jamaica Plain — see *Roxbury*.

Lenox Street. *Yellow car* — on Tremont St., or
Scollay Sq., or *Belt Line car*, West.
See Locations **1, 4, 14**

Longwood. *Blue car* — on Tremont, or Boylston
Sts. See Locations **4, 6, 7**

Magoun Square—see *Somerville*.

Malden.

VIA FERRY STREET, EVERETT. *Amber car*—via Charlestown.   See Locations **1, 5, 21, 28**

VIA WEST EVERETT. *Amber car* — via Charlestown.   See Locations **1, 5, 20, 21, 28**

VIA WINTER HILL. *Amber car* — via Charlestown.   See Locations **1, 5, 25**

Marlboro Street. Take any Brookline, Reservoir, Allston, or Back Bay car from Tremont House, except Huntington Ave.   See Locations **1, 4**

Medford, via Malden. *Amber car* —via Charlestown, Everett, or West Everett.
          See Locations **1, 5, 20, 21, 25**

Medford Square, via Winter Hill. *Amber car*— via Charlestown.   See Locations **1, 5, 25, 32**

Meeting House Hill. *Dark Blue car* — from Franklin St., via Washington St. and Mt. Pleasant, to Upham's corner and Geneva Ave.
          See Locations **7, 8**

Milton. *Dark Blue car* — from Union Station, via Washington St. and Dorchester Ave., and from Franklin St., via Mt. Pleasant Route.
          See Locations **8, 17**

Mount Auburn. Take any Mt. Auburn, Newton, or Harvard Sq. car, free transfer from latter at Harvard Sq.   See Locations **2, 13**

Neponset. *Dark Blue car*—from Franklin St., via Washington St., via Mt. Pleasant route to Field's Corner and Adams St., to Neponset.
          See Locations **8, 17**

Newton. *Crimson car* — Bowdoin Sq., and Cambridge route.   See Locations **2, 13**

Newton Corner. Terminus of West End Co's *Crimson car*, connecting with Newton St. Ry. Co's cars for Newtonville, West Newton and Waltham.
          See Locations **2, 13**

Newtonville. *Scarlet car* — from Watertown to Newton Upper Falls and Echo Bridge. *Crimson car*—from Newton to Waltham. See—*Newton.*

Newton Upper Falls. See Echo Bridge. See *Newton.*

North Cambridge.

NORTH AVENUE. Take any Cambridge car (except Pearl St.) and transfer at Harvard Sq., or North Ave. and Arlington car. See Locations **2, 13**

PORTER'S STATION. *Red car*—from Bowdoin Sq. See Location **2**

SPRING HILL. *Crimson car* — marked *Union Sq.* See Locations **1, 5, 11, 24**

Norfolk House. *Green car*—from Union Station, via Washington St., and terminates at Old Heath St. See Locations **5, 8**

Oak Square — see *Brighton.*

Old Heath Street — see *Roxbury.*

Park Square and Providence Depot. Terminal and central point of several routes. See Locations **9, 11, 13, 23, 24, 25**

Pearl Street and Putnam Avenue — see *Cambridge.*

Porter's Station — see *North Cambridge.*

Prospect Park — see *Waltham.*

Quincy. HOUGH'S NECK. See *Quincy Centre.* See Location **41**

Quincy Centre. *Amber car*—to Neponset, Quincy Point and East Weymouth, West Quincy and Manet Beach, or Hough's Neck. East Weymouth and the Beach, 10 cents, remainder, 5 cents. See Location **41**

Quincy Point. Cars from Neponset, Quincy, or East Weymouth, a pretty summer resort on the South Shore. 8-cent check from Neponset. 5 cents from other points. See Location **41**

Reservoir — see *Chestnut Hill.*

Rowe's Wharf. *Yellow car* — from Roxbury Crossing, West Lenox St., Tremont and Summer Sts. *Green car*—on Washington and Summer Sts. and Atlantic Ave. *Red car* — from Union Station, via Causeway and Federal Sts., to Kneeland St.
See Locations 2, 8, 10, 11, 14, 15

Roxbury.

GROVE HALL. Take any Cross-town or Grove Hall car.
See Locations 1, 4, 5, 6, 7, 8, 9, 11, 16, 25, 26

JAMAICA PLAIN. *Lemon Yellow car* — at Union Station, Scollay Sq., or Tremont St.
See Locations 1, 4, 5, 11, 14

OLD HEATH STREET. Terminus of " Norfolk House " and East Boston Ferry routes, and reached by cars of Jamaica Plain route.
See *Norfolk House* and Locations 1, 4, 8

Roxbury Crossing. *Yellow cars* — for Jamaica Plain, or Old Heath St., via Tremont St.
See Locations 1, 4, 8, 12, 15

Scollay Square. Boston is known as the Hub of the Universe, of which Scollay Square is the axle or pivot, the radiating and distributing point of trade and travel.
See Locations 6, 7, 16, 18, 20, 21, 22, 23, 25

Somerville.

CENTRAL ST. *Red car* — on Charles St., or Craigie's Bridge, via Somerville Ave.
See Locations 1, 4

FRANKLIN ST. *Amber car*—via Charlestown from Boylston St.   See Locations 3, 8

MAGOUN SQUARE. *Amber car*—from Scollay Sq., via Charlestown.   See Locations 1, 5, 25

UNION SQUARE, via Cambridge. *Crimson car* — from Scollay Sq. to Spring Hill, North Cambridge.   See Locations 1, 5, 11, 23

UNION SQUARE, via Charlestown. *Amber car* — on Washington St., north from Temple place to Warren Bridge.   See Locations 4, 5, 8, 9, 25

South Boston.

BROADWAY. *Red car* — from Harvard and Park Sq. See Locations **6, 8, 11**

CITY POINT. *Red* or *Crimson car.* Locations **1, 3, 4, 5, 6, 8, 10, 11, 13, 18, 23, 24**

DORCHESTER STREET. *Red car* —via Washington St. from Union Station. Transfer Station (free) at West Broadway, near City Point. See Locations **8, 11**

Spring Hill — see *North Cambridge.*

Summer Street — see *Cambridge.*

Tremont Street. Boston's great artery of travel, entering from Scollay Square to Roxbury Crossing. See Locations **9, 10, 11**

Union Square — see *Somerville.*

Union Station. From whose tracks more trains are despatched than from any other passenger Depot in the world, and at or near whose entrance, street cars pass. See Locations **1, 2, 3, 4, 6, 8, 9, 10, 12**

Upper Falls — see *Newton.*

Waltham. PROSPECT PARK. Terminus of *Crimson car* of Newton St. Ry Co. The point of land in the vicinity of Boston first sighted by mariners approaching Boston Harbor. See *Newton.*

Western Avenue — see *Brighton.*

West Everett. *Amber car*—on Scollay Sq., Cornhill to Warren Bridge and Charlestown. † See Locations **5, 9, 11, 20, 21**

West Medford. 5-cent ride to Malden or Medford Sq.

West Newton. Near Waltham beyond Newtonville. See *Newton.*

West Quincy. *Amber car*—at Neponset, Quincy, Weymouth, or Quincy Point. See Location **41**

West Roxbury. FRANKLIN PARK. Take any Grove Hall car.
See Locations **1, 4, 5, 6, 7, 8, 9, 11, 16, 25, 26**

Winchester. Cars from Woburn and North Woburn to Symm's Corner, and in summer to Medford Sq. 5-cent ride from either point. See Location **32**

Winter Hill — see *East Somerville.*

ROUTES OF LYNN & BOSTON R. R.

Street Railways from Distant Points not yet Connected with Boston.

Amesbury — see page 51.

Annisquam — see *Gloucester.*

Asbury Grove — see *Hamilton.*

Asylum Station — see *Danvers.*

Bass Rocks — see *Gloucester.*

Bay View — see *Gloucester.*

Beach Bluff Avenue — see *Lynn.*

Beachmont — see *Revere.*

Belt Line Circuit — see *Lynn.*

Beverly.

BEVERLY COVE. Cars from Town House Sq., Salem, via Beverly to Chapman's Corner, Hale St. Five-cent ride from Salem.   See Locations 37, 39

GLOUCESTER CROSSING. Terminus of cars from Wenham, Salem, Peabody and Danvers. Route of cars to Beverly Cove. Five cents from Salem or Wenham.   See Locations 37, 39, 40

Brier Neck — see *Gloucester.*

Central Square — see *Lynn.*

Chelsea.

CHELSEA SQUARE. Terminus of " Through Line " from Woburn, Stoneham, Melrose, Malden and Everett. All cars from Marblehead, Swampscott, Lynn, Revere and the Beaches pass here to and from Scollay Sq. Five cents from Boston. See Locations **1, 9, 29, 31, 32, 33, 34, 35, 36**

Chelsea — *continued.*

WASHINGTON AVENUE. *Cream colored car* — from Scollay Sq. branching to the left at Bellingham from Broadway. Five cents from Boston.
See locations **1, 9, 30**

Cliftondale — see *Saugus.*

Crescent Beach — see *Revere.*

Danvers.

DANVERS CENTRE. *Lemon yellow cars* from Marblehead to Asylum Station, and *Maroon cars* from Salem via Peabody, pass here. Ten cents to Marblehead, five cents to other points.
See Locations **37, 38, 39, 40**

ASYLUM STATION. Terminus of *Yellow cars* from Danvers. Salem. Marblehead. Fifteen cents from Marblehead; ten cents from Salem; five cents from Danvers.   See Locations **37, 38**

PUTNAMVILLE. The home of General Israel Putnam and terminus of *Maroon cars* from Salem and Beverly via Peabody. Five-cent fare from Peabody or transfer from Asylum Station. Ten cents from Salem.   See Locations **37, 39, 40**

DANVERSPORT. Route of North Salem, Danvers and Marblehead cars. Five-cent ride from Danvers; five-cent ride from Salem.   See Location **37**

Dedham — see page 51.

Everett.

WOODLAWN CEMETERY. *Cream colored cars* from Scollay Sq. via Washington Ave. Five-cent fare from Boston.   See Locations **1, 9, 30**

Framingham, South — see page 51.

Franklin Park — see *Saugus.*

Glenmere — see *Lynn.*

Gloucester — see page 51.

ANNISQUAM — see page 51.

BASS ROCKS — see page 51.

BAY VIEW — see page 51.

Gloucester — *continued.*

BRIER NECK — see page 51

EAST GLOUCESTER — see page 51.

LANESVILLE — see page 51.

Hamilton.

ASBURY GROVE. Terminus of cars from Wenham and Camp Ground of M. E. Society. Summer line only. Five-cent ride from Wenham.

See Location 39

Haverhill — see page 51.

Highland Circuit — see *Lynn.*

Hyde Park — see page 51.

Lakeside — see *Lynn.*

Lanesville — see *Gloucester.*

Lawrence — see page 51.

Lewis Street — see *Lynn.*

Linden — see *Revere.*

Lowell — see page 51.

Lynn. *Cream colored cars* from Scollay Sq. through Charlestown, Chelsea, Revere and Saugus Marshes to Lynn, and beyond to Swampscott and Marblehead.

See Locations **1, 9, 29, 30, 31, 33, 37, 38, 40**

BEACH BLUFF AVENUE. The dividing line between Swampscott and Marblehead is near here, and is nine miles from the boundaries at Cliftondale, or Saugus and Melrose line, which is a five-cent ride by transferring at Central Sq., and a five-cent ride from Revere and Saugus line.

See Location of *Marblehead* cars.

BELT LINE CIRCUIT. *Crimson car,* seven miles continuous ride, five cents. Take car at any point. From South St., Western Ave., Eastern Ave., Brookline to Chatham St., Bloomfield St. to Gold-

Lynn, BELT LINE CIRCUIT — *continued.*

fish Pond, Chestnut, Howard and Friend to Silsbee and Mt. Vernon Sts., Central Depot. Exchange and Broad to Revere Beach Depot and Market St., State, Pleasant and Wheeler to Blossom St., and Alley, Commercial and Neptune Sts. to South St.

CENTRAL SQUARE. The " Castle Garden " or " Scollay Square " of Lynn. If you want a steam or electric car, barge or herdic. Central Sq. is your place. Five-cent ride from all points in the city, Saugus (except No. Saugus). and Swampscott See Location all cars marked *Lynn.*

GLENMERE, VIA MAPLE STREET. *Emerald green cars,* route same as Lakeside, entering Essex St. via Ireson St., and taking Maple St. from Chatham St. to the left. Five-cent ride.
See Locations 35, 36

HIGHLAND CIRCUIT. *Scarlet car* with Tartan band, circling from Central Depot to the rear of old High Rock. and returning via Market St. Five-cent ride. See Locations 35, 36

LEWIS STREET. Route of Swampscott and Boston cars, terminus of *Lemon yellow cars* from Myrtle via Walnut and Washington Sts. Five-cent ride.
See Locations 34, 35, 36

LAKESIDE. *Emerald green car* from Myrtle St. near Breed's Pond, and via Boston. Franklin and Market Sts., Broad and Union Sts., Mason and Essex to Chatham St. and Euclid Ave., around Flax Pond to Pickering School and Sluice Pond. Five-cent ride. See Locations 35, 36

LYNNHURST. Terminus of *Maroon cars* from Central Sq. to No. Saugus boundary, connecting with *Amber cars* for Wakefield, Reading, Melrose and Stoneham See Locations 34, 36

LYNN WOODS. Route Wyoma from West Lynn and Great Woods road. Five cents from Lynn or West Lynn. See Locations 34, 35, 36

Lynn — *continued.*

MYRTLE STREET. *Emerald green cars* to Glenmere and Lakeside, via Franklin and Chatham Sts. See Locations **35, 36**

NAHANT BEACH. Terminus of cars from Central Depot, and *Yellow line* from Myrtle St. via Walnut and Washington Sts., and by transfer from all five-cent routes except Belt Line. See Location **36**

WYOMA. *Light blue cars* from Lynn Common Station via Market St. to Central Depot, and Union and Chestnut Sts. to Broadway and Wyoma Sq. Five cents from West Lynn or Peabody. See Locations **34, 35, 36, 40**

Malden.

MAPLEWOOD. Route of *Yellow cars* for the Beach and Malden cars to Lynn. Five cents to Malden or Linden : ten cents to Lynn; Malden to Lynn, ten cents ; Malden to Cliftondale, five cents ; Malden to Linden, five cents ; Malden to Revere Beach, ten cents; Malden to Boston via Revere, ten cents. See Locations **29, 36**

MALDEN SQUARE. *Lemon yellow* to Maplewood, Linden and Revere Beach, ten cents. *Maroon cars* to Lynn and Upper Swampscott, via Maplewood, Linden, Franklin Park and Cliftondale, ten cents. To Chelsea, Everett and Melrose, five cents ; Stoneham and Woburn, ten cents. See Locations **29, 30, 31, 32, 33, 36, 37**

PINE BANKS PARK. Malden and Melrose boundary and route of cars from Woburn to Chelsea, local transfer (free) from cars of Lynn and Salem line, after crossing boundary of Saugus and Melrose. See Locations **29, 30, 31, 32, 33**

Maplewood — see *Malden.*

Marblehead — see *Lynn cars* and Locations **1, 9, 30, 34, 35, 36, 37**

Melrose. Five-cent ride from Malden, Stoneham or Saugus. Ten cents from Lynn, Swampscott, Woburn or Chelsea. Fifteen cents from North Woburn, Winchester, Salem or Boston, via Chelsea. Boston to Melrose, ten cents, via West End from Malden.
See Locations **29, 30, 31, 32, 33, 36**

MELROSE HIGHLANDS. On route of cars from Melrose to Stoneham and Woburn. Free transfer on cars from Saugus boundary to Melrose (Lynn and Salem line).
See Locations **29, 30, 31, 32, 33, 36**

Natick and South Natick — see page 51.

Newburyport — see page 51.

Norfolk and Suburban St. Ry. -- see page 51.

Peabody. *Scarlet car* — via Broad and Exchange St. to Central Depot, Andrew and Market Sts. to Essex St., and Washington and Boston Sts. to Broadway, Wyoma, and Boston, Washington and Main Sts. to Peabody Sq. Ten cents from Lynn; five cents from Danvers or Salem.
See Locations **35, 36, 37, 39, 40**

Pine Banks Park — see *Malden.*

Plum Island — see page 51.

Putnamville — see *Danvers.*

Rockport — see page 51.

Reading. *Amber cars* from Wakefield, Stoneham, North Saugus, Melrose and Lynn, five-cent ride from Wakefield.   See Location **33**

Revere.

BEACHMONT. *Light green cars* from Scollay Sq. via Beach St., Revere. Five-cent ride.
See Locations **1, 9, 30**

CRESCENT BEACH. *Maroon cars* from Scollay Sq. via Chelsea and Revere to Western Ave. Five-cent ride.   See Locations **1, 9, 30**

Revere — *continued.*

LINDEN. On route Lynn and Malden cars, and Revere Beach line from Malden, and free transfer from Boston at Revere St., and five cents from Malden, Cliftondale or Boston.

See Locations **29, 30, 36**

REVERE BEACH. By transfer (free) from Lynn cars at Revere St.; or in Summer by car from Scollay Sq. Fare, five cents from Boston.

Salem.

TOWN HOUSE SQUARE. The business center of Witch City, at one time the Liverpool of New England. Five-cent ride to Beverly, Peabody. Ten cents from Lynn, Wenham or Asylum Station and Danvers.

See Locations **29, 33, 36, 37, 38, 39, 40**

SALEM WILLOWS. *Maroon cars* from Town House Sq., Salem, via Essex St., Block House Sq. and Fort Ave. to Salem Neck. Five-cent ride or free transfer to or from city limits. See Locations **37, 40**

Salisbury Beach — see page 51.

Saugus.

CLIFTONDALE. Route of *Maroon cars* from Lynn to Maplewood and Malden. Five-cent ride from Lynn or Malden. See Locations **29, 36**

EAST SAUGUS. Route of cars to Lynn from Saugus Centre to Melrose, and Cliftondale to Malden.

See Location **36**

FRANKLIN PARK. Trotting Park near route of cars from Lynn to Malden. Five cents from Malden; ten cents from Lynn. See Locations **29, 36**

NORTH SAUGUS. *Amber cars* from Lynn boundary to Wakefield, five-cent ride.

See Locations **33, 34, 36**

SAUGUS CENTRE. Route of *Maroon cars* from Salem via Lynn and East Saugus to Melrose. Fare, fifteen cents from Salem; five cents from Lynn; ten cents from Melrose.

See Locations **33, 36, 37**

Stoneham. Terminus of Wakefield and Stoneham R. R. line, route of Chelsea and Woburn cars. Five-cent ride to Woburn, Melrose or Wakefield, or via Wakefield to Melrose.

See Locations **29, 30, 31, 32, 33, 37**

Swampscott — see *Lynn cars* and Locations **1, 9, 29, 30, 33, 34, 35, 36, 37, 38**

LOWER SWAMPSCOTT. *Cream colored cars* to Marblehead, Lynn, Revere, Chelsea and Boston. Fifteen cents or two for twenty-five cents from Boston or Chelsea; ten cents from Revere; five cents from Lynn or Marblehead.

See Locations **1, 30, 34, 35, 36, 38**

UPPER SWAMPSCOTT. *Maroon cars* to Salem, Lynn, Cliftondale. Linden, Maplewood, Malden, Saugus and Melrose, connecting with Woburn and Chelsea line. Five cents from Cliftondale or Lynn or from the Saugus and Melrose boundary, nine and one-quarter miles.

See Locations **29, 33, 36, 37**

Town House Square — see *Salem.*

Wakefield. *Amber cars* — from Lynn line via North Saugus, Stoneham, Melrose and Reading.

See Locations **33, 34, 36**

Washington Avenue — see *Chelsea.*

Wenham. Terminus of cars from Beverly and Hamilton Camp ground, five-cent ride.

See Locations **37, 39**

Woburn. Terminus of through line from Chelsea, connecting with Lynn and Salem at Melrose. Route of North Woburn, Winchester and Medford line. Fares to Lynn and Chelsea, fifteen cents; to Everett and Malden, ten cents; Boston via Medford, fifteen cents; Salem, Marblehead and Boston via Chelsea, twenty cents.

See Locations **29, 30, 31, 32, 33, 36, 37**

Woodlawn Cemetery — see *Everett.*

Wyoma — see *Lynn.*

APPENDIX.

GLOUCESTER STREET RAILWAY CO.

First Division. From B. & M. Station, through Main St. to East Gloucester, a distance of three miles or more. Fare, five cents ; time, thirty minutes.

Second Division. Starting from Main St. passing the B. & M. R. R. Station through Washington St., past the villages of Riverdale, Annisquam and Bay View to Lanesville. Distance, seven miles ; fare, ten cents ; time, forty-five minutes. In connection with these, an extension is under way from a point near Bass Rocks to Brier Neck. a distance of about three miles, following the shore toward Rockport. .

HAVERHILL AND AMESBURY STREET RAILWAY.

Haverhill to Amesbury, fare, twenty cents ; distance, twelve miles. Amesbury to Newburyport, fare, ten cents ; distance, ten miles. Amesbury to Salisbury Beach, fare, ten cents ; distance, ten miles. Newburyport to Plum Island, fare, ten cents ; distance, three miles.
.

LOWELL, LAWRENCE AND HAVERHILL STREET RAILWAY.

Lowell to Lawrence, fare, fifteen cents ; distance, ten miles. Lawrence to Haverhill, fare, ten cents ; distance, nine miles.

NATICK AND FRAMINGHAM STREET RAILWAY.

South Natick to Natick, five cents. Natick to South Framingham, five cents.

NORFOLK AND SUBURBAN ST. RY.

Soon to be connected with the West End St. Ry. at Forest Hills, running from Dedham through Hyde Park.

In Lynn Woods with Pen and Camera.

Finely illustrated. By Hon. NATHAN M. HAWKES. one of the Park Commissioners.

Cloth, $1.25 ; half leather, $2.00

Patriotic Selections for Memorial Day.

Compiled by Miss HARRIET L. MATTHEWS and Miss ELIZABETH E. RULE of the Lynn Public Library.

School edition, 50 cents

Campaigning with Banks and Sheridan.

By FRANK M. FLYNN. Personal Reminiscences of the war for three years. . . . . Cloth, $1.25

Map of Lynn Woods.

Published in pocket form. . . . . 15 cents

Studies of the Essex Flora.

The Flora of Essex County, Mass. By CYRUS MASON TRACY. Second revised edition. Cloth, $1.00

Where to Go — How to Get There.

A guide of electric car routes radiating from the City of Boston: also places of interest and amusement. By T. W. PRESTON. . . . . 25 cents

Studies in the Beginnings of Christianity.

For Sunday Schools. By J. M. PULLMAN, D. D. Special rates to Sunday Schools.

PUBLISHED BY THE NICHOLS PRESS,

THOS. P. NICHOL

LYNN, - - MASS.